DATE DUE			

A New True Book

THE COMMONWEALTH OF INDEPENDENT STATES

By Karen Jacobsen

Consultant: Abraham Resnick, Ed.D.
Professor of Social Studies Education
Jersey City State College
Jersey City, New Jersey

ℙ CHILDRENS PRESS ®

CHICAGO

A Russian musician shows off his balalaika, an instrument like a guitar.

PHOTO CREDITS

Photri—Cover Inset, 4 (top), 9, 15 (left), 21 (main picture), 24, 31 (2 photos), 37 (right), 42, 44 (left), 45 (center); © Mauritius/D. Weber, Cover; © Inis Kalnins Press Studio JV, 11 (left); © Martti Kainulainen, 11 (right), 13 (right); © AISA, 13 (left), 29 (2 photos), 30, 32 (2 photos), 33, 35 (right), 36 (2 photos), 38, 39, 40 (2 photos); © Ari Ojala, 15 (right); © SALMER, 37 (left)

Reuters/Bettmann—18

Bob & Ira Spring—17, 23 (left), 27 (left), 44 (right), 45 (right)

SuperStock International, Inc.—© A. Tessore, 16 (left); © Kurt Scholz, 16 (right), 22 (right), 45 (left); © AGE Spain, 21 (inset); © Steve Vidlet, 22 (left); © Ken Proctor, 26; John Strohm, 27 (right); © Owen Lattimore, 35 (left); © Herbert Lanks, 41

TSW-CLICK/Chicago—© Cliff Hollenbeck, 2, 44 (center); © Alan Smith, 14; © Karen Sherlock, 23 (right)

Valan—© M.G. Kingshott, 25 (2 photos)

Maps by Len Meents—4 (bottom), 7 (large map)

Maps by Horizon Graphics—7 (globe)

COVER: Moscow, Red Square with Kremlin and St. Basil's Cathedral
COVER INSET: Typical Russian wooden house

Project Editor: Fran Dyra
Design: Margrit Fiddle

Library of Congress Cataloging-in-Publication Data

Jacobsen, Karen.
  The Commonwealth of Independent States / by Karen Jacobsen.
    p.   cm. — (A New true book)
  Includes index.
  Summary: Discusses the collapse of the Soviet Union and the resulting Commonwealth of Independent States formed by some of the former Soviet republics.
  ISBN 0-516-02194-X
  1. Commonwealth of Independent States—Juvenile literature. [1. Commonwealth of Independent States.] I. Title.
DK1.5.J33 1992
947—dc20   92-12946
                                 CIP
                                 AC

95-547

TABLE OF CONTENTS

The Alain Valley in the Pamir Mountains of Tajikistan
On the map below you can see the fifteen republics
that once were part of the Soviet Union

Latvia

Estonia

Lithuania

Belarus

Ukraine

Moldova

Russia

Georgia

Armenia

Azerbaijan

Kazakhstan

Turkmenistan

Kyrgyzstan

The Union of Soviet
Socialist Republics (USSR)

Tajikistan

Uzbekistan

THE END OF
THE SOVIET UNION

The Soviet Union was the world's largest country. It stretched from Europe all the way across Asia to the Pacific Ocean.

The Soviet Union had 290 million people living in fifteen republics. It had a central government, and it was led by powerful Communist dictators. The government had complete control over daily life in every Soviet republic.

But, in December 1991, the Soviet Union came to an end. In its place there were fifteen free and independent states: Armenia, Azerbaijan, Belarus, Estonia, Georgia, Kazakhstan, Kyrgyzstan, Latvia, Lithuania, Moldova, Russia, Tajikistan, Turkmenistan, Ukraine, and Uzbekistan.

The Commonwealth of Independent States

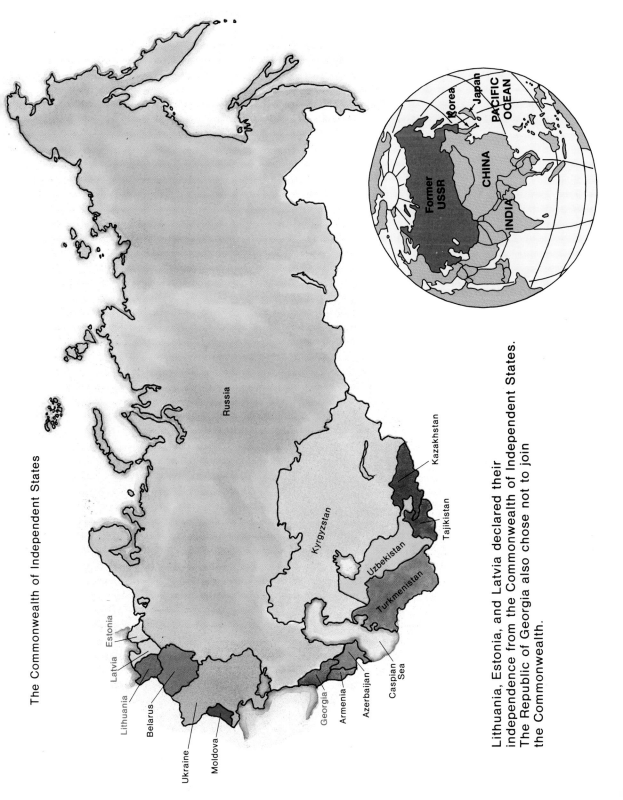

Lithuania, Estonia, and Latvia declared their
independence from the Commonwealth of Independent States.
The Republic of Georgia also chose not to join
the Commonwealth.

TROUBLE IN THE SOVIET UNION

For more than sixty years, the Soviet Union was a major power among the nations of the world. But in the 1980s, things began to go wrong. Failures and disasters weakened the power of the Soviet government.

In 1985, Mikhail Gorbachev became the head of the Soviet Union. He tried to solve the

Mikhail Gorbachev (left) talking to workers
at the Likhachev Auto Works in Moscow

problems. First Gorbachev
introduced *glasnost*–the
free and open exchange
of ideas and information.
Glasnost allowed the
Soviet people to learn
what was happening in
their country and in the
other parts of the world.   9

Next, Gorbachev introduced *perestroika*– reforms that changed the government and the economy. These reforms gave the Soviet people a chance to choose their own leaders. In 1989, the Soviet Union had its first free elections.

President Gorbachev wanted to make the Soviet government more free. He wanted to keep the Soviet Union from splitting apart.

But the new leaders in

Latvians (left) and Estonians (right) celebrate their independence
after more than fifty years of Soviet rule.

some of the republics had
other ideas. Lithuania, Estonia,
and Latvia declared their
independence. They left
the Soviet Union.

By the end of 1991, all
of the Soviet republics,
including Russia, had left.
Mikhail Gorbachev had
become a president
without a country.

11

THE BALTIC NATIONS

Lithuania, Latvia, and Estonia are all European nations with ports on the Baltic Sea. In 1940, all three were forced to become republics in the Soviet Union. But they never stopped trying to get their independence back.

In March 1990, Lithuania became the first Soviet republic to try to quit the Soviet Union. The Soviet

The city of Vilnius, Lithuania (left). Lithuanian schoolgirls (right) in their school uniforms

government decided to punish Lithuania. The Soviets cut off all oil and gas shipments to the republic. Without fuel, the Lithuanian people suffered, but they did not give up.

Today, Lithuania is free. Its capital is Vilnius.

13

The independent nation of Latvia is a center for trade. Its important industries are shipbuilding and fish-canning. Latvia's native people are called Letts. There are also many Russians and Germans living in Latvia. The Latvian capital is Riga.

Riga, a port city on the Baltic Sea, is the capital of Latvia.

Tallinn (left) is
Estonia's capital.
People sell
flowers on the streets
of Tallinn (above).

The people of
independent Estonia live
well. They produce dairy
goods and manufacture
other valuable products.
Estonians are known for
their music, arts, and crafts.
Tallinn is Estonia's capital.

15

GEORGIA

Georgia is a mountainous nation east of the Black Sea. It produces manganese, coal, iron, and timber. Its farms grow grain, tea, citrus fruits, and tobacco. The Georgian people have their own language and writing. They

Lake Riza in Georgia (left) is surrounded by the Caucasus Mountains. A tea plantation (right) near Batumi, Georgia.

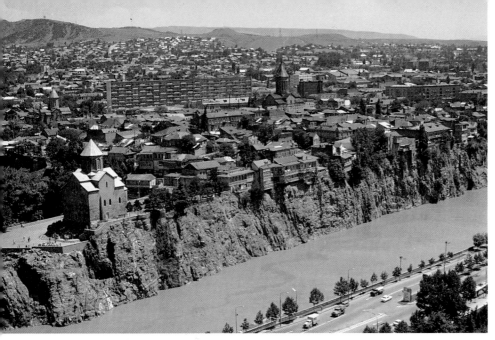

The Metekhi Church in Tbilisi, Georgia, was built in the fifth century.

are Christians. The capital of Georgia is Tbilisi.

In 1992, just after Georgia became independent, its president was forced out of office. Today, Georgia is run by elected officials who are trying to bring more democracy to the republic.

17

Hundreds of thousands of people demonstrated in support of Russian president Boris Yeltsin in Moscow on February 24, 1991.

JOINING TOGETHER

In December 1991, the leaders of Russia, Ukraine, and Belarus held a meeting. They talked about their common interests and problems. On December 8, they decided to form a new family of nations called the Commonwealth of Independent States—the CIS. Soon eight more former Soviet republics—Armenia, Azerbaijan, Kazakhstan, Kyrgyzstan, Moldova, Tajikistan, Turkmenistan, and Uzbekistan—joined the Commonwealth.

Each Commonwealth state has its own government and makes its own laws.

At first, the purpose of

the CIS was to stand together against the central government. But now the CIS works to find fair and peaceful ways to share the property—and solve the problems—left over from the central government of the Soviet Union.

Georgia may join later, but the Baltic nations—Lithuania, Latvia, and Estonia—do not want to join the CIS.

Sheep herding and horse breeding are important in Kyrgyzstan.
Lake Baikal in Siberia (inset) is more than 5,000 feet deep.
It is the deepest freshwater lake in the world.

RUSSIA

Russia is the largest nation in the CIS. It stretches from the plains of eastern Europe across Siberia to the Pacific Ocean. It extends from the Arctic Ocean in the north to China in the south.

21

Modern buildings in the city of Moscow. The Bolshoi Theatre
(inset) is one of Moscow's famous landmarks.

Russia has more than
150 million people. Its
cities, industries, and arts
are very advanced.
Moscow, its capital, was
the capital of the Soviet
Union.

Because Russia is so

large and has so many

Sunbathers (left) enjoy the warm summer climate of a
resort on the Black Sea. Women dressed for a cold winter
in the northern Russian city of St. Petersburg (right)

different nationalities within
its borders, someday its
people may want to divide
into several nations. The
other CIS nations are
careful to make sure that
Russia doesn't try to take
over and tell them what to
do.

BELARUS

Belarus is a small European nation east of Poland and south of Lithuania. Like Russia, Ukraine, and parts of Moldova, it is a Slavic country. Belarus, also known as White Russia, is a land of forests and farms. Its factories

This factory in Minsk, Belarus, employs women to assemble delicate instruments.

24

Public buildings in Minsk, Belarus. At the top is the town hall.

manufacture automobiles, textiles, tools, and other products. Minsk is the capital of Belarus. The governments of Russia, Ukraine, and Belarus met in Minsk to form the Commonwealth.

25

The harbor at the Ukrainian port city of Odessa
in the Crimea, a peninsula on the Black Sea

UKRAINE

South of Belarus is
Ukraine, a large European
nation with ports on the
Black Sea. For many years
the Ukrainian people felt
like prisoners in the Soviet
Union. They wanted to be
free to run their own country.

26

Ukraine has some of Europe's finest farmland. Its chief crops are wheat, sugar beets, and potatoes. It also produces large amounts of dairy products. Ukraine has rich supplies of coal, iron, and other minerals. Kiev is its capital city.

Kiev, once the capital of the Russian empire, is now the capital of Ukraine. Ukrainian farmers (inset) stack hay.

MOLDOVA

Between Ukraine and Romania lies the small nation of Moldova. It used to be part of Romania. But in 1948, Moldova was forced to become part of the Soviet Union. The Moldovan people speak Romanian and use the Roman alphabet. In Russia and most other CIS republics, the Cyrillic alphabet is used. Many Moldovans would like their nation to

Harvesting wheat (left) on a Moldovan
farm. Moldovan folk dancers (above)

become part of Romania
again.

Moldova's farmers raise
fruit and vegetables. Its
factory workers produce
textiles and electrical
equipment. The Moldovan
capital is Kishinev.

ARMENIA

To the south of Georgia lies Armenia. Armenian farmers grow figs, grapes, and other crops. Its factories produce textiles, chemicals, and machines.

Vineyards in the Ararat Valley of Armenia

Splashing fountains (above) line a street in Yerevan, Armenia.
A monument in Yerevan (top right) commemorates
Armenian victims of Turkish massacres during World War I.

The Armenian capital is
Yerevan.

Most Armenians are
Christians. They are not
friends with their Muslim
neighbors in Turkey and
Azerbaijan. For many years
the two groups have
fought against each other. 31

AZERBAIJAN

Azerbaijan is a small nation on the Caspian Sea. Its people speak a Turkic language and are Muslims. Azerbaijan has rich supplies of oil, iron ore, and cobalt. Its

An oil refinery (left) and a vineyard (right) in Azerbaijan

The Icheri-Shekher Palace in Baku, Azerbaijan's capital, is now a museum.

farmers raise wheat, cotton, fruit, and tea. An important export product is caviar—fish eggs from sturgeon caught in the Caspian Sea. Baku is the capital of Azerbaijan.

THE CENTRAL ASIAN NATIONS

There are five Commonwealth nations in Central Asia—Kazakhstan, Kyrgyzstan, Tajikistan, Turkmenistan, and Uzbekistan. The people of these nations primarily speak Turkic languages and follow the Muslim religion.

Kazakhstan is the second largest Commonwealth nation. It stretches from the edge of

Left: A Kazakh woman.
Right: Harvesting wheat on a
farm in northern Kazakhstan

Europe eastward to the border of China. Kazakhstan's native people are Kazakhs. Many are shepherds who tend their flocks on horseback. Other Kazakhs grow wheat, sugar beets, and tobacco on the rich soil of the steppe.

Alma-Ata (left).
The spaceship *Soyuz 22* (right)
stands on the launch pad
at the Baikonur Cosmodrome.

Half of the nation's people are Russians or Ukrainians. They came to live in Kazakhstan when it was a Soviet republic. Baikonur Cosmodrome, which was the space center of the Soviet Union, is in Kazakhstan. Alma-Ata is the capital of Kazakhstan.

To the south of Kazakhstan is Uzbekistan. The people are Uzbeks. Uzbek farmers grow cotton in irrigated fields. Nuts and dried fruits are also produced. The nation has rich supplies of oil, coal, copper, and sulfur.

Irrigation canals carry water to the fields in Uzbekistan (left). The Chimgan Mountains (below) are now being developed as a resort area outside Tashkent.

Tashkent is the largest city in the Central Asian republics.

Tashkent, Uzbekistan's capital, is an important Muslim center.

Turkmenistan, a dry desert land, is west of Uzbekistan and north of Iran. Turkmen farmers grow cotton and corn in irrigated fields. Shepherds raise sheep for wool to weave into thick Oriental rugs. Turkmenistan's mines produce coal, sulfur, gypsum, salt, and some gold. The capital is Ashkhabad.

An oil well in Turkmenistan

Sheep-herding in Kyrgyzstan (above). A young
Kyrgyz woman (right) picking cotton

Kyrgyzstan is a
mountainous land on the
border of China. The
Kyrgyz people came from
Mongolia. Many Kyrgyz
farmers raise tobacco,
cotton, rice, and sugar
beets. Its factories produce
40 textiles, chemicals, and

modern appliances.
Bishkek is the capital of
Kyrgyzstan.

Tajikistan is a small
nation in the Pamir
Mountains between China
and Afghanistan. The
Tajiks have the same
culture and language as

Tajiki girls weaving rugs

The city of Dushanbe, Tajikistan, with the
Himalaya Mountains in the background

the people of Iran. Many
Tajiks are shepherds or
carpet-makers. Some grow
crops on hillside farms.

Tajikistan produces coal,
natural gas, and oil. The
capital of Tajikistan is
Dushanbe.

WILL THE COMMONWEALTH LAST?

The Commonwealth of Independent States is very shaky. Some of its nations are large and powerful. Others are small and weak. Some are European. Others are Asian. Some are longtime friends. Others are old enemies.

In their meetings the nations argue with one another. Some even try to

Left: A farmers' market in Yerevan, Armenia. Center: Crab fishing in Russia. Right: Uzbek man at a public market in Tashkent

tell the others what to do. There is danger that the Commonwealth may break apart–just as the Soviet Union did. Meanwhile, as long as it lasts, the CIS has important work to do.

The work of the Commonwealth is not easy.

Left: Russian woman in traditional dress. Center: A couple in Bukhara, Uzbekistan. Right: Uzbek woman in the public market at Tashkent

Each nation wants to protect itself–to gain and not lose. By talking, by trading, by working together– the Commonwealth nations may be able to keep peace and improve the lives of all their people.

WORDS YOU SHOULD KNOW

caviar (KAV • ee • yar) — the eggs of the sturgeon, a large fish

citrus fruits (SIH • truss FROOTS) — fruits such as oranges, lemons, and limes

cobalt (KO • bawlt) — a shiny gray metal used in making inks and paints

commonwealth (KAHM • un • welth) — a group of independent nations that join together to help one another

Communist (KAHM • yoo • nist) — a system of government under which all businesses are owned by the state and the people's lives are controlled by the leaders

copper (KAH • per) — a brownish-red metal used in electric wires

Cyrillic alphabet (sir • RILL • ik AL • fa • bet) — the alphabet used in writing Russian and some other Slavic languages

democracy (dih • MAH • krah • see) — rule by the people; a system of government in which the people elect their leaders

dictator (DIK • tay • ter) — a ruler who has complete power over the people of a country

economy (ih • KAH • nuh • mee) — the system by which people get the things they need and want, such as food and clothing

exchange (ex • CHAYNGE) — to give something in return for something else

glasnost (GLASS • nost) — the free and open exchange of ideas and information

gypsum (JIP • sum) — a powdery white mineral used in making plaster

independent (in • dih • PEN • dint) — not controlled by another person or country

irrigated (EER • ih • gay • tid) — watered with water brought from nearby rivers or lakes through ditches or canals dug by people

manganese (MAN • guh • neez) — a grayish metal

Oriental rugs (or • ee • EN • til RUGZ) — valuable rugs woven from pure wool in colorful patterns

perestroika (pair • ess • TROY • ka) — reforms in the government and the economy

republic (rih • PUB • lik) — a country with elected leaders who make the laws and run the government

Slavic (SLAH • vik) — a member of a group of people in eastern and southern Europe who have similar languages and background

steppe (STEP) — a large grassy plain where there are few trees

sturgeon (STER • jun) — a large food fish

sulfur (SUL • fer) — a pale yellow substance that is used in making matches and medicines

Turkic (TER • kick) — a group of languages spoken by many peoples living in Turkey, across Central Asia, and in western China

INDEX

About the Author

Karen Jacobsen is a graduate of the University of Connecticut and Syracuse University. She has been a teacher and is a writer. She likes to find out about interesting subjects and then write about them.